CW00863886

THE 4 ELEMENTS
AND
MEDITATIONS

EARTH, WATER, FIRE AND AIR

VIRGINIA RAY LONG

Copyright © 2013 by Virginia Ray Long
All rights reserved.

ISBN: 1490390111
ISBN-13: 978-1490390116

First Edition, First Publishing: 2013

Table of Contents:

Acknowledgements

My many heartfelt thanks to everyone that I have met in my life, for all of you that have contributed to my growth. Angels appear when least expected and in the most unexpected forms. You all know who you are. I honor you and bless you for your gifts.

We all have friends - some come in and out of our lives, and some that are with us through out our lives. They support us, encourage us, and help us grow. Marilyn Du Mont, Lyn Hammond Gray, Jennifer Boose, Sally and Lucia are my co-travelers on the earth plane. You have accepted me for who I am. You have encouraged and supported me with all of my unique-ness.

My husband, the love of my life – you let me be me. I love you for that. And, my 'pets' that teach me unconditional love. I honor and bless you all, always and forever.

PROLOGUE

> I don't think God cares where we were
> graduated or what we did for a living.
> God wants to know who we are.
>
> Discovering this is the work of the soul –
> It is our true life's work.
>
> ~ *Bernie Siegel*

Greetings Journeymen,

The early years of my life were spent growing up near a State Park with a huge gorge that provided a river with many waterfalls and trees and forests and countless places to hike and wander and wonder. I would listen to stories about the Indians and how they lived off the land; and how they honored the sun and moon and all things good. I would camp with my family in wooden cabins and cook out over open fires and look for 'fuzzie wuzzies' hiding behind the trees. It was a wonderland of investigation for me. Then, I went to school and growing up got in the way. Because of that extraordinary start in life, I have always felt curious of the whys' and hows' of nature and the elements. Air, fire, water and earth are the basic elements of the Universe. They are the building blocks of everything.

As an adult on vacation, I fell in love with Hawaii. It felt like 'home'. And, the native people told stories about living off the land, about honoring the land and the water and the animals and the sun and the moon. It was very similar to the stories I heard as a child, about the Indians.

Between childhood and vacations to places that honor the land, and seasons and sun and moon, I had a life with family, friends, loved ones and career. Yet, there always felt like something was missing. Somewhere there was a disconnect. Now, as I approach this new phase of life, I have made the time to reconnect. It seems that everything I study brings me back to the four elements and how they relate to everything in my life. EVERYTHING.

Next, it took me years to understand meditation. For me, the most difficult part was to get rid of the "mind chatter". I still work on it. Because of that, I found it easier for me to focus on 'something' to get the mind to quiet the chatter. Then, I decided to create my own meditations around things I wanted to discover with my inner mind. From that, I found a way of expression and discovery. The next step was to bring this all together; the wonderment of my childhood, learning from my 'walking meditations', to putting this together in writing and creating guided meditations about the four elements and how they intertwine with life, and living, and the physical body and of ALL.

It is my pleasure to share my discovery with you. This study will continue as long as I live on this Earth. It is my hope that these will inspire your own journey of discovery.

INTRODUCTION

For me, writing is always a time of great challenge. I write, I review, I re-write, I throw away and start over. Eventually, something is created. To create a written document adds another dimension to any experience. It makes it real. It is a written document of one's perspective of something important. It is demonstrating one's filter of how they see the world. What a beautiful thing to share!

This work has helped me view my own filter in another light. And, the magic is that it changes each time I read it, or do the meditations. There is another perspective, outlook or idea that shows itself. Just like the circle of life, never ending, never beginning, and always moving and always in motion.

To me, the meditations are a support system. When I need balance or inner strength, I usually go to the chakra meditation that I feel I need at the time. When I need a different perspective in something outside of me, I usually go to the element meditation that I feel will help for more clarity. They allow me to "open up" to new ideas or a new awareness of life around me. Being open to change is a gift.

Each time I spend time outside with the elements, it is a joy, a wonderment, an 'a-ha' moment. If I cannot get outside, I can use these creations to go inside, to learn, to grow, to ask for guidance. And, each time I do this, I learn, I grow, I find guidance.

CHAPTER 1 – IN THE BEGINNING

Two of many things I have learned in my years of self-study.

1. We learn by two methods, observation and experience. We watch and observe our family (parents, siblings, grandparents, cousins); then, we either become them or the complete opposite. When we get hurt, like putting your hand on a hot stove, the experience teaches us we don't want to do that again. It is interesting to watch children. They learn by observing the things that happen around them. Then, they do those same things to discover the reaction to those actions. I wonder, does that ever really change throughout life? Are we not all children inside forever?

2. "Where were you at ten years of age?" There is a theory that part of that 10 year old stays with us. What was happening to you at ten? If you were ten during the Great Depression, it may be hard for you to spend money, or be frivolous. If you lived in NYC during 9/11 – what emotions would hide inside a ten year old? This is food for thought when interacting with others. What was happening to them at the age of 10?

I did not live through either of those experiences, but I do remember what was happening to me at ten. I was miserable. I had no idea of what was happening to my body, but I did know that it was changing rapidly. I was VERY self-conscious and had very low self-esteem, for a variety of reasons. It was not a fun place for me. And, I was sure I was the only one that had these issues. Everyone was smarter, or prettier, or more athletic, or faster, or talented, etc, etc. It only took about 40 years to overcome those silly thoughts. I am still refining some of the old patterns that sometimes creep back in. The good news is that now, in the present time – those thoughts rarely sneak through. If they do, I don't feel them anymore, they just roll by.

Every ten year old is learning independence, is very impressionable, and the brain is still soaking in everything! What was life like for you at fifth grade?

At this point in life, the most important thing I have learned is that   everything starts from within. You cannot expect others to love you, if you do not love yourself first.

For me, this was quite difficult. It was much easier to avoid that inner self and pretend to live life as some stranger I thought I should be; someone I had to pretend to be so I could be happy, or successful, or to have friends. That did not work for me. This is my story.... Not the story of my life, but my journey to happiness, peace and harmony and contentment. At this point in life, I love my life and I love what I am doing and I love who I have become.

The place to improve the world is first in one's own heart and head and hands, and then work outward from there.   ~ Robert M. Persig

CHAPTER 2 – KNOW THYSELF

In 1651, Thomas Hobbes, (The Leviathan) was responding to a popular philosophy at the time – and said that you can learn more by studying others than you can from reading books.

He said that one learns more by studying oneself: particularly the feelings that influence our thoughts and motivate our actions. To paraphrase – he said look into one's self and consider what does he think, opine, reason, hope, fear, etc … and upon what grounds; he shall thereby read and know what are the thoughts and passions of all men upon like occasions.

In 1711, Alexander Pope wrote a poem entitled "An Essay on Man, Epistle II", which begins "Know then thyself, presume not God to scan, the proper study of mankind is Man."

In 1750 Benjamin Franklin, in his Poor Richard's Almanac, observed the great difficulty of knowing one's self, with: "There are three things extremely hard - Steel, a Diamond, and to know one's self."

In 1831, Ralph Waldo Emerson wrote a poem entitled ('Know Thyself'), on the theme of 'God in thee.' The poem was an anthem to Emerson's belief that to 'know thyself' meant knowing the God which Emerson felt existed within each person.

This is a message to Mother Earth that I share before a meditation circle.

A message to our Earth Mother:

Whenever we meet in ceremony,

We meet in a safe place to celebrate your spirit.

We meet in freedom.

We meet in your presence,

For you are the celebration of joy.

Your ONLY law is love unto all.

You are the secret of birth, the mystery of life.

Beyond death, you give peace and reunion with

those gone before.

You are the soul that gives life to the universe.

From you all things proceed and unto you all

things return.

May this worship be in the joyous heart,

For all acts of love and pleasure are yours.

Let there be beauty and strength,

Power and compassion, honor and humility

With each and every day of life.

As we seek to know you, we understand always

We will achieve nothing until we unlock the

mystery:

For whatever we seek:

If we do not find it inside, we will never find it

outside.

Whatever you want, look inside first –
happiness, joy, peace, or contentment....
So I did.

Next, step, looking inside –

CHAPTER 3 – MEDITATION

Meditate instead of medicate!

Meditation is one of the keys to understand Life - your life. From the world I was born into and spent the formative years, meditation was a foreign word. Not only did I have a chatterbox brain, I also had that ten-year-old brain that had to be re-programmed. And, that is work. How does one start to meditate? The 3 P's.

1. Practice
2. Persistence
3. Patience

There is a saying, "Fake it until you make it". It works well in many situations. Learning to meditate is one of them. Put your thoughts in a box. Put them on rose petals and let them drift down the stream. Free your mind of 'chatter'. Whatever works for you, just do it until it works. It is one of those things that "When you know, you know." You can practice and practice and practice and still wonder if it is working yet. Then, all of a sudden, one day – you got it!! It is not something you can explain, you just know. If you think you know, you don't know yet.

"When you know, you know."

~ Rayism (from Rev. Reggie Worrell)

Sounds easy. I find the easy things are the hardest to accomplish. It took me years to get there. Sitting and waiting for my mind to clear did NOT work. Then, I discovered that when I would go for a walk, I could "lose myself" in the walk, ideas would come flowing to me. Well, I did this for a long time before it hit me – this is a form of meditation. Let the thoughts 'go away' and let the mind flow... I knew I had found a way to meditate. "When you know, you know."

One day, as I was losing myself in my walking meditation time, I began another journey of teaching myself about our connection with nature, Mother Earth. We need the plants and trees for survival. We need them to exist. Back to ten years of age, again – in General Science, we learn about plants.

The photosynthesis conducted by land plants is the ultimate source of energy and organic material in nearly all ecosystems. Photosynthesis radically changed the composition of the early Earth's atmosphere, which as a result is now 21% oxygen. Animals (including humans) are aerobic, relying on oxygen. Plants are the primary producers in most ecosystems and form the basis of the food web in those ecosystems. Many animals rely on plants for shelter as well as oxygen and food.

I learned about this in basic science class, yet now I began to see the 'connection' in new light. We all need each other to survive. The plants feed us and we feed the plants.

That thought wandered to elements that are the basis all things – air, fire, water and earth. It is the basic composition of us all and all around us. How are we intertwined with the universal elements?

CHAPTER 4 – THE ELEMENTS

What is an element? (Dictionary)

1. One of four substances, air, fire, water, or earth formerly regarded as a fundamental constituent of the universe.

2. A substance composed of atoms having an identical number of protons in each nucleus. Elements cannot be reduced to simpler substance by normal chemical means.

I began my study of the four fundamental universal elements of Air, Fire, Water and Earth. It is possible to find these in many rituals, religions, writings, philosophies, etc. They may have various titles, yet they are there, the building blocks of life... (Building balance in our lives).

This is my daily prayer to the elements:

Stand and look to the EAST, with open arms –

As I look to the East, it is the morning sun; it is
the promise of a bright new day.
Come to me Air, so fresh and so clean
Grant me the wisdom to be sharp and keen,
Send me creativity and clarity, too.
Bring positive thoughts to all that I do.
By your fragrant breath, the air
By winds blown cold and breezes fair
Cleanse and clear my body clean,
Blow away all negativity.

Turn to the SOUTH.

As I look to the South, it is the noonday sun; it is
the heat of the day, full of passion and power.

Come to me Fire, so warm and so bright,
As I walk through life, my pathway do light.
Send me passion to live with pure zest
Standing up for truth when put to the test.
By the passion of her soul's desire

By dancing flames and burning fires
Cleanse and clear my body clean,
Burn away all negativity.

Turn to the WEST.

As I look to the West, it is the setting sun. It is the twilight of the day, time for reflection and review.

Come to me Water, flowing and free
Grant me compassion and tranquility
With Life's ups and downs, let me smooth
With all the issues, help me soothe.
By the water that runs through her veins,
By raging rivers and gentle rains
Cleanse and clear my body clean
Wash away all negativity.

Turn to the NORTH.

As I look to the North, it is the midnight sun. It is the time of death, renewal, and re-birth, as we prepare for a new day.

Come to me Earth, so rich and so moist,
Grant me serenity, peace and joy
Send me stability and ethical ways
So I may help others the rest of my days.
By the solid Earth with her body round
By mountain, valley, hill and mound.
Cleanse and clear my body clean,
Take away all negativity.

When I do this, I think of the circle of life, a
continuous loop: a moment in time, a day, a
week, a year, a lifetime – the medicine wheel.

Examples:

- Air, Fire, Water, Earth
  -
- Morning, Noon, Evening, Night
  -
- Begin, Peak, Complete, End
  -
- Spring, Summer, Autumn, Winter
  -

- Baby, Adult, Senior, Elder
  -

All connected, all part of the divine;
All part of the cycle of life.

NOTE: I was directed to do the elements in this order, EARTH (physical), WATER (emotional), FIRE (spirit) and AIR (mental), It moves from the physical experience to the ethereal, most to least dense.

CHAPTER 5 – MEDITATIONS – CHAKRAS AND The ELEMENTS

In my study of the elements, I cherish each one for what they give us. It has brought balance into my life. It has brought acceptance into my life. It has brought contentment into my life. It has brought living into my life. This had also made me enjoy where I am in life and how each part has added to the whole. I start with Earth. It is the most solid, stable element. It represents the body, a physical manifestation of the soul. It is our support system. As you read through this section, Earth is the preparation for the new breath, new day, and new life – the preparation for the beginning!

ഗഗഗഗ

EARTH – North – Winter

The Physical Body

We can survive WEEKS without food.

(4 – 10 weeks), maybe

In winter, the trees have shed their leaves, the harvest is gone, and the sun time is short. In nature and in our lives it is the time for introspection as we prepare for a new year. At Halloween, we celebrate the final harvest and the food collected to get us through the winter months. At Thanksgiving, we give thanks for that food. At Christmas time, we celebrate the return of the sun, as the days start to increase once, again. In the Corporate World, it is the completing sales, finalizing current budgets, and preparing new budgets.

Definition for EARTH: (Dictionary)

1) The fragmental material composing part of the surface of the globe
2) The sphere of mortal life as distinguished from spheres of spirit life (heaven, hell)
3) Areas of land as distinguished from sea and air, the solid footing of soil
4) The planet on which we live that is third in order from the Sun
5) The people of the planet Earth, the mortal human body, the pursuits, interests and

pleasures of earthly life as distinguished form spiritual concerns.

Affirmation:

Come to me Earth, so rich and so moist,
Bring me serenity, peace and joy
Send me stability and ethical ways,
So I might help others the rest of my days.

BY THE SOLID EARTH WITH HER BODY ROUND,
BY MOUNTAIN, VALLEY, HILL AND MOUND.
CLEANSE AND CLEAR MY BODY CLEAN
TAKE AWAY ALL NEGATIVITY.

About:

This is the element of the material, physical and sensual. In its negative presentation it can seem plodding and unimaginative, concerned with only the task at hand. It is the element of manual labor, service and submission, but also of fertility and the source of all fruitfulness. It represents the "material" possessions, money and physical "things".

Astrology: Earth

The earth element represents matter. You can touch it and often see or hear it. Earth is real and physical because it is perceivable by the five senses.   For anything to manifest, it must contain the elements earth or water. Of all the elements, the earth element is the most easily to confine and capture, to hold in the hand. It is rigid, fixed and stable. Anything that is attainable is "down to earth".   It is the foundation of all that is. Like the real earth, it is fixed, stable, organized and predictable. It is limited and disciplined.

Of all the elements, it is the earth that can be possessed and owned. It provides a solid basis for our existence (dependable and stable), yet it can rise only so far. And the higher it rises (a boulder on a mountain), the farther it has to fall, making it cautious.

Earth people are cautious, premeditative, conventional and dependable. They live by a practical, common sense code and seek physical wellbeing rather than spiritual enlightenment. The expression "down to earth" sums them up. They are responsible, methodical, and concerned with detail. Children of the earth element are therefore well suited to life on this planet. They are realistic, builders and hard workers. They reduce everything to what is practical, useful and observable. They particularly value skills and abilities. Earth types are successful business people in the sense that they can stably maintain things. While the fiery type is an innovator, the earth type is cautious and practical, being more interested in established business activities than new innovative ones. They think about what is, rather than what might be. In a way, they lack imagination. They can be too fixed to rules, regulations and procedures.

Chakras:

The word comes from the Sanskrit, meaning "wheel, circle", and sometimes also referring to the "wheel of life". They bring energy to the body and are physical, mental and vibrational in nature. They are considered centers of life force energy.

Earth represents the first, or Root Chakra – it is vitality, survival, and our connection to Mother Earth. It is related to security, survival and also to basic human potential. It is said to relate to the inner adrenal glands, responsible for the fight and flight response when survival is under threat.

NOTE: Before meditation it is important to find a quiet place where you will not be disturbed, take 3 deep breaths to relax the body, the mind, and the spirit.... Take a few moments to settle into a peaceful place. READ SLOWLY and absorb the message, pause often.

MEDITATION: Root Chakra

As you sit, imagine a dual coil of vibrant energy embracing and dancing around your spine and body. As one spiral comes down from above and fills body with the spirit of life; there is another spiral to pull up the power of earth to meet the light above. Imagine your entire existence as a reflection of the balance and play of these two energies, flowing and glowing, on and in and around your body. And, breathe. Be sensitive and aware of all thoughts and feelings that may arise as you gently allow the energy center to open, and flow, and swirl. As you proceed – previous blocks and past issues may release to your awareness. Accept whatever happens, reject nothing, surrender yourself, and enjoy experience. Let us begin.

Let the tips of your thumb and index finger touch as you allow awareness to move to the first energy center located at the base of your spine. Focus your attention at the base of your spine. Perhaps you may quietly hum or think, "LAM".

As you allow awareness to linger there with no purpose, expectation or intention; the gentle thoughts begin to stimulate this area at the base of your spine and your hips and a slow circular motion begins, as a warm flow of pulsating energy emerges. Notice a deep clear RED light begin to appear, as pulsating waves radiate to each and every cell of your body, enriching it with peaceful, warm, vitality.

Surrender completely to this pulsating stream of power as it flows to and around and through you. Sense this area opening more and more, allowing life of Earth energy to enter your body.

Follow this energy to its source, deep down to the core of the Earth. It flows with the intense color Red, the color of vitality and movement and blood. A continuous stream of energy arises from innermost part of Mother Earth and flows to you. Experience this hidden power continuously flowing from within the Earth. Your body is formed by this power and is constantly nourished by it. This is the very same energy that forms the planet and plants and animals. The same life force that created all on Earth - pulsates through you. Feel it flowing into your body – the red color of vitality circulating through your body with every breath. Sheltered within power of the Earth you are protected, nourished, and shielded by this glorious vibrant energy. As it increases, keep your attention on this powerful energy at the bottom of your spine. Focus at the base of the spine and imagine that with each breath, the energy collects and builds there. Continue to relax and sense the feelings deep inside. Breathe as if the earth's energy is coming directly into you from below. You are born of this Earth. The Earth is what you are. The color is red. Smell the Earth. Feel the cool dirt. Feel the density of your bones and support structure of your body. You are at the beginning, the child. Reality is physical. Like the infant, you identify with the body. You experience yourself at the center of everything.

You love to eat and sleep. You fear pain and death. Your sole purpose is self-preservation. Allow yourself to acknowledge your "dark" side and your potential for "small-mindedness", for it is the necessary lesson of this level of existence. Understand yourself as a child of animal instincts and primitive tendencies. Fully accept that you are a creature of habits and needs and you are rooted in the earth. As you continue to breathe in and out through this center, allow your body to begin to feel that you are in a safe place. Allow yourself to feel secure and safe and comfortable enough to let go of protection and relax. You may repeat to yourself the following affirmations.

"Here and now, I feel safe. I am protected. I am loved. "

- I am balanced and grounded to the Earth.
- I am ready to release old habits that no longer serve me.
- I am willing to accept myself and others.
- I love life and I love living and I love me.

Bathe in this clear, red vibration – feel it flow in and around and through your body - let this vitality blend, meld and circulate for a while. Take your time to pause and enjoy the moment.

And, now it is time to return, to this place and time and day. Bring yourself back slowly. When you are ready, open your eyes.

ଔଔଔଔ

Meditation on the Element of Earth*

You have decided to take a journey to the element of Earth.

You find yourself at the edge of a forest and discover an open path. The evening sky stretches overhead with stars sprinkling across the heavens. You ask permission to enter as you breathe in the fragrance of the Earth and notice the richness of the path under your feet.

The forest grows thick around you as you venture in. The dark silhouettes of cedar, birch and fir trees reach up to the sky. As you look up, you notice a faint green aura surrounding them. You go to an ancient pine tree and place your hands on the trunk. You press your ear against the bark and listen. The sap is rising; you hear and feel the movement of life within the tree. The tree creaks as it sways in the wind. It is hundreds of years old. It holds ages of wisdom. As you slide your hands down the trunk, there are thick leaves covering the base of the tree. The aroma of the sour, tangy earth scent fills your nostrils.

You continue on the path. There are faint noises as critters dart in and out of the forest. There is a deer gazing at you from the bushes. Then, with the faint shadow of wings, a bird soars into the sky.

As you continue, the forest falls away as the path moves upward. Walking up a dry, barren hill now, there are patches of grass scattered at your feet. Your legs begin to ache. Your breath becomes difficult because the incline is steep. The small, dark opening at the top of the hill is your destination and it keeps you moving. You stretch with both hands and feet to reach the last part of the trail. Along the cliff there is one last pull to grab the ledge.

You rest for a moment near the opening that leads into the mountain. The ledge is firm, and wide enough to sit. There is the legend of the Earth King who lives deep within the sacred mountain. It is the story of his crystal palace that sparkles with energy that captured your interest. You want to learn about the power of the earth and the strength and wisdom that live at the core of the Earth.

Rested – you stand and take a deep breath, then enter the side of the mountain. As the darkness gives way to the dim shadows, there is a faint sparkle of light on the walls. It lights your path just enough for you to see. You run your fingers across the stone. A faint shimmer of light twinkles on your skin; this is the faerie fire, the fire with no heat. It glows green and gold in the dark.

A cough startles you. In front of you stands a little person, shorter than your knee. He is sturdy and dressed in brown and green and a long beard extends from his chin. He wears a cap of moss and carries a twisted cane in his hand. He looks at you, his eyes are the dark brown of the dirt, "I will take you to the inner kingdom of the Earth. I am your guide. I will take you to the King of the Earth who lives at the center of the world." With that, he leads you down a narrow, sloping passage. It would be easy to slip, so you must be careful as you follow the little one.

The journey is long and silent. After some time, the little man stops and points to the cavern wall. There are earth and stone patterns in the wall. "People once lived here. They made things from the earth, from clay and wood and stone. This is what was left behind. Someday these remains will dissolve back into original elements. Touch one of the pieces; feel it. Let it talk to you. And, listen."

As you pass through the layers of time, there are pictures drawn in stone on the cavern walls. As the journey continues you notice a skeleton that lies locked in the soil. You hear a voice, "The flesh has long gone back to earth; the bones take longer. They are the roots of this world. Look at the bones, and then look at your own hands. Understand that inside your body, your own skeleton stands strong. It is your roots, holding you together. Understand that each person has his time and then returns to the earth. You may return to life many times, but each time, your body returns to the soil."

When you think you can go no further, when your legs ache, you hear, "We are almost there. Look for the opening ahead. It leads across a river of lava to the palace of the king." And as suddenly as he appeared, the little man is gone.

A sense of anticipation rushes over you. From where you stand, you hear the beating of drums. It echoes through the very stone beneath your feet.

You are at the edge of a great cavern; so vast you cannot perceive the other side. In front of you there is a flowing river of lava. It boils and twists, rushing past you. There is a narrow stone archway with steps leading up to it. This is a bridge that you must pass over. On the other side, there is a crystal palace. It sparkles in the light from the river of molten fire. There is a glimmering, shimmering, and sparkling of amethyst and emerald and citrine and ruby and sapphire. You climb the stairs to the arch. The stone bridge is narrow. It has a thin, yet sturdy rail to hold you. As you cross the bridge, the lava sizzles and crackles beneath your feet.

Once on the other side, there is a descending staircase. You are close to the palace door. It swings open as you approach. The drumming noise grows louder. As you approach the quartz archway, you realize that the drumming noise is your very own heartbeat matching the rhythm with that of the vibration of the Earth.

Once inside, one gigantic room fills the entire palace. In the center is a throne of granite and quartz. On top sits a life form. He is huge, with skin as knobby as bark, muscles carved out of wood and a face as ageless as the Earth from which he draws his power. This is the Earth King, The Ruler of the North.

He looks at you and says, "I am the King of Earth. I serve the Great Mother. You are here to learn the mysteries of the soil."

He gives you a basket. "Look inside." In the basket you find a blade of grass, a slender oak branch, an apple, a bone, a crystal, a lump of earth, a flower, and a piece of fur.

"Hold the blade of grass. Examine it, feel the sharp edge, look at it. It is the hair of the

Goddess; break it and smell it. Run it through your teeth. Now take it – hold it - feel its vibration."

"Next, take the oak branch. Hold it. Feel the strength that resides within the wood. Hold it, close your eyes and envision the tree from which it came. The oak is the root of the world; it is the strongest and most sacred tree. Feel its vibration."

"This is so marvelous; so wonderful, Mother Nature in all her beauty. Now take the apple and bite into the fruit, taste the sweetness. This is provided for you."

"Now look at the bone; it is the stone of your body and reminds the world that you were here. But it, too, passes as time goes by."

"The crystal condenses the powers of the Earth. Each stone contains a different essence. And, now take the fur. All animals are an extension of the Earth, as are trees and rocks and bodies - all interconnected, all physical."

"Pick up the bowl of earth. Smell the rich, vibrant, fertile soil that grows all fruits and livestock to sustain your body. Without the dirt beneath your feet, there is no life. Without the soil, you would not exist."

You look up into his swirling eyes, eyes as green and vibrant and brilliant as emeralds. You look into that ancient face that contains wisdom, compassion and an ever-present core of iron and steel. Remember, you are looking into a mirror, for all life is intertwined and every tree and every flower is a reflection of you.

"Now take the flower; look in its center and envision the mystery of Earth, of beauty caught in physical form. Inhale, and learn what it is you came here to learn. This is my gift to you."

As you look into the flower, the aroma surrounds you, bringing with it strength and grace and beauty. Draw the essence of the flower into your soul and listen.

The King smiles at you "You must return to the outer world. There is a staircase behind me; it will lead you back. Go now and remember what you have learned." And, he sends you on your way.

You find the staircase. The railing is strong, the stairs are wide and smooth and easy and carved of vibrant, shimmering crystal.

As you climb the stairs, they turn from clear crystal, to granite, then to bone. As you begin to notice, the stairs turn to tree roots, you feel alive and alert. Notice the light coming from above, the stairs turn to oak, then grass, and then there is a door – as you go through the door you are back to the forest – where you began. Take a moment to soak in the journey. When you are ready, bring yourself back to this day, this time, and this room and open your eyes. Welcome back.

ଢଢଢଢ

The Earth is not just soil and dirt. It is a living, breathing organism. The best thing we can do to help Mother Earth is to help ourselves. As we improve, so does the earth. It is the least we can do for her – after all, she gives us life. As above, so below.

Questions:

What have you learned from these meditations?

How will you look at the element of Earth differently?

How will you look at yourself differently?

What has changed?

Will you do anything differently?

How do you feel the Earth element works inside of you?

What thoughts do you have about the Root Chakra?

When do you think is a good time to sit and be with the "Root Chakra"?

When do you think it would be helpful to "pull in" the energy of the root chakra?

How could that help you in life situations?

ﬖﬖﬖﬖ

WATER – West – Autumn

The Emotional Body

We survive DAYS without water.

(4 - 8 days)

In autumn, we have completed the long days of fun in the sun. The harvest has provided us with food and joy and camaraderie. The days are getting shorter. It is now time to reflect on our success (the harvest, career, love, life). It is time to review our successes and challenges. In the Corporate world – busy bringing in business to complete the fiscal year.

Definition of WATER: (Dictionary)

1) A liquid that descends from the clouds as rain. It forms streams, lakes and seas and is a major constituent of all living matter. When pure, it is an odorless, tasteless, slightly compressible liquid oxide of

Hydrogen (H_2O) which appears bluish in thick layers, freezes and 0 ^{C} and boils at 100 ^{C}. It has a maximum density a 4 ^{C} and high specific heat. It is ionized to hydrogen and hydroxyl ions, and is a poor conductor of electricity and a good solvent. It changes according to the temperature surrounding it.

Affirmation:

Come to me Water, flowing and free
Grant me compassion and tranquility
With all ups and down, help me smooth
With all of life issues, help me soothe.

BY THE WATER THAT RUNS
THROUGH HER VEINS
BY RAGING RIVERS AND GENTLE RAINS
CLEANSE AND CLEAR MY BODY CLEAN
WASH AWAY ALL NEGATIVITY

About:

Water represents the emotions, the creative impulse and the subconscious. It is the "inner voice" of our intuition and primal brain that our more rational selves attempt to ignore. It is also present in the more "walled off" aspects of our personality as well. Water is the element of emotional excesses, and dreaminess (even unto "flakiness", one could say), it has the potential to displace air, to drown out fire, and to turn earth to consumptive mire. On the other hand, it is the source of all life on the planet and all organic life is predicated on its presence. Certainly without the "interest" of emotion, creativity and subconscious processes, our lives would be more than a little dull. Similarly, according to Jung, it is through the subconscious that we gain access to the universal "collective" super conscious.

Astrology: Water

Water, like earth, is heavy, and falls. It is less easily constrained than earth, but more than fire or air. Water can rise up into the air (although it falls again as rain). Like earth, it has form. It is less limited than the earth, but more limited than fire and air. While fire cannot be contained, it disappears if you totally enclose it, and air expands to fill any container, water is more limited and keeps its volume, and has a level. While fire cannot destroy the earth, water can. Water can rise high with the help of air, but generally doesn't move upwards. Water is extremely powerful, and will always find its own level. If artificially constrained at a high level, it will eventually break free, but then it will fall. Water is impressionable and reflective. It can go deep. It refers to the inner mind.

Normally water absorbs energy. It takes in the energy of others. Water is more sensitive than the other elements in that it can appear in the three forms of matter: solid like the earth; liquid - its normal state - and as vapor - like air.

Water people are very sensitive to their own feelings and those of others. They perceive life through their emotions. They are concerned with what feels right, their impressions, rather than with what is rational. They use the emotions, not the intellect, to understand and to value. Water can raise people to the heights of bliss, but can bring them down to the depths of despair.

Water rises into the air and falls as rain, nurturing the land. The earth absorbs it to become fertile. Living things need water. With it they grow and mature. Without it they die.

Water people need close emotional relationships. They can be volatile. They are romantic, sentimental and affectionate. They can be nurturing and possessive with their family. They have fixed opinions. They communicate in non-verbal ways; emotionally, psychically, or through forms as art, dance, music, poetry and photography. Their beliefs are based on feelings rather than on reason, passion or practicality.

Chakra:

Water represents the second chakra, or Sacral Chakra. It is movement and fluidity. Here it represents our emotional flow, feelings, and openness. "Go with the flow" is an excellent motto for this chakra. It is the focal point of our emotions, sexuality, and creativity. It governs our sense of self-worth, how we relate to others, and our self-confidence of our own creativity.

NOTE: Before meditation it is important to find a quiet space, a few deep breaths to relax the body and calm the mind.... Take a few moments to settle into a peaceful place. Read SLOWLY, and pause often.

MEDITATION: Sacral Chakra

As you sit, imagine a dual coil of vibrant energy embracing and dancing around your spine and body. As one spiral comes down from above and fills body with the spirit of life; there is another spiral to pull up the power of earth to meet the light above. Imagine your entire existence as a reflection of the balance and play of these two energies, flowing and glowing, on and in and around your body. And, breathe. Be sensitive and aware of all thoughts and feelings that may arise as you gently allow your energy centers to open, and flow, and swirl. As you proceed – previous blocks and past issues may release into your awareness. Accept whatever happens, reject nothing, surrender yourself, and enjoy the experience. Let us begin.

While the pulsating power of Earth begins flow to you, let awareness gradually drift to the area just below the navel. Place your hands in your lap, palms up, on top of each other – left hand underneath and thumbs gently touching. Perhaps, you can quietly think or hum "VAM".

Become aware of the energy circulating without purpose, expectation or intention. Your awareness stimulates this area of lower abdomen, sense the subtle circulating waves. It feels like swirling warm water, evolving and dancing with steady flow of gentle energy.

At the center, a clear orange light begins to grow; it intensifies with each turn of the circulating motion; it's a purifying stream of the lymphatic system. Your body is now a single flow of living, vivid orange energy. Allow the power generated below to surge upwards and spread out at this area, just like warm orange lava, flowing out of a volcano.

The natural element is water; it is mutable and not easily contained. You are pulled by the power of the moon and swayed by your own emotional tides. The flow of moisture begins to soften the earth from below; it becomes fluid and the energy of movement develops.

Notice your desires awakening. Tune into any sensation of vibrating movement and allow it to gradually grow, while breathing and centering on this power within you, the most powerful force in the universe. Allow the flow of energy to expand, casting out to pores of your skin, surrounding and bathing and enfolding you in its gentle strength, soothing, sustaining you gently rocking you as if you were child.

The sea is all around you, as the stream of life permeates you within. Your internal sea bathes and heals the cells in your body. Surrender to this rocking water of light. Your body and soul release knots as this purifying source of light increases.

Channels open forgotten memories and awaken those ancient inner feelings. From all directions around life flows open - soothing and caressing you with energy. The vibrant stream of life expands, growing into the warm water, lovingly supporting you with rocking motion, surrounding you with its golden orange rays.

You may feel your own creativity expanding and coming to your awareness.

Waves of light open, as the horizon shows a golden light of sun with orange rays bathe you in a deep and intimate way. You realize this beam that flows through you also flows through each and every living thing. Full of confidence, you surrender to this flow. Receive and celebrate the vibrations and the rhythms of life. Recognize yourself, with your very own unique, personal, creative powers.

You may repeat the affirmations:

- I am in the flow of my life.
- I am in tune with my emotions.
- I am able to surrender and neutralize my fears.

- I am alive and joyful.

- I forgive the past.

- I release sacrifice from my life.

- I do what I chose for my own well-being.

- I choose to love myself unconditionally.

- I am entitled to happiness and health and joy in my life.

- I acknowledge my mistakes and re-affirm my self-esteem.

- I deserve the best for my life.

Bathe in this clear, orange vibration. Let it flow in and around and through your body - let this orange light blend, meld and circulate for a while.

And, now it is time to return, to this place and time and day. Bring yourself back slowly. When you are ready, open your eyes.

಴಴಴಴

Meditation for the Element of Water*

You decide to journey to the element of Water. It is an overcast day. You find yourself near a forest of tall, dark pine trees. It has been said that somewhere deep within this forest is a beautiful water garden. You have decided to venture into the forest to find the cavern of water. You find a path that runs into the forest. Along the path there is a meandering stream. You stand at the side of the bank, looking down into the ravine shaded by thick fern and long, hanging moss.

You begin walking the path and following the stream alongside. The path is old and cluttered. Fallen logs are covered with moss and large chunks of rock are obstacles along the way.

As you enter the forest, the heavy growth filters the light of the sun, as day fades into twilight. The sounds of birds echo around you, and a cool breeze chills the air with a hint of the cold night to come. The stream rushes along beside you. At first the ravine is steep, and you cannot feel the spray of the water. Yet, you can feel the dampness of being near the water. Gradually the slope lowers to only a few feet above the water. You can see clearly below the surface of the water if you bend down. There are small fish that dart across the surface of the bubbling water, and a few mosquitoes hover over the tide pools.

The walking is easy at first. It is cool near the stream, almost chilly, and sometimes you can hear the little critters that live nearby. Then, the forest thickens as you focus on the stream below. Occasionally there is laughter that rises from the water, yet you can't tell from where it comes.

The current begins to move faster, and you feel a sense of urgency, inspired by the force of the water. You try to keep pace with the water. Then, up ahead, you see a large boulder blocks the path, making it impossible to continue along the river's edge. If you detour off the path, you may lose the pathway to the water garden. There is one other option. You could let the water carry you. It is deep and swift and it would work. So you step forward and jump into the water.

The first shock of the ice cold water stuns you. You flounder for a moment, fighting the current that drags you past the boulder. You catch your breath, straighten out, and then ride the current. You do not have to swim; just stretch out and let the waves carry you.

The last little light of the sun glistens on the water. It sparkles like brilliant blue sapphires, dazzling your eyes. You are soaked, yet find yourself adjusting; it is easier to remain calm now, easier to stretch your arms out in front of you and steer yourself around the occasional rock jutting up from the water.

The pulse of the current begins to match your heartbeat as a strong quiver runs through you. With each breath you take, the stream seems to rise and fall with the movement of each in and out breath. As you exhale, the stream lowers, and you gently but swiftly flow along, almost as if you were a part of the water itself.

The large, dark boulder towered overhead. At this point, there is no turning back. The only choice is to let the water guide you. Suddenly thirsty, you open your mouth and let some water slide down your throat. The icy water refreshes you like no other drink ever before.

A roaring sound echoes up ahead, and again the water picks up speed. You raise your head to see what is coming; yet it is difficult to see. Suddenly, you find yourself teetering on the edge of a waterfall. All you have time for is a glimpse of white water mist spraying all around you before you plunge over the edge.

Twisting, and turning, you manage to find that you are actually sliding down a waterfall, balanced by the force of the cascading water. You catch a glimpse of a glistening pool below, and the fern covered area surrounding it, just before you hit the surface and sink.

Every time you swim upward, kicking and fighting all the way, you grab another breath; then again you are pulled back below the surface. You are spinning now, and each time you break the surface, you gain a breath of air; it is hard to pull free from the whirlpool.

The water encompasses you, tearing at your clothes, stripping away any possessions you might be carrying. When you think you have reached your last gasp, you manage one final kick and push yourself out of the whirlpool to a place where you can break free. With this last bit of energy, you swim to shore and crawl onto the sand. You find you are naked; your clothes have been swept away, and all possessions are gone. You are so tired; you just sit and rest.

As you regain your strength, the cold seeps into your bones. Your skin is dry. The night air is so cool you begin to shiver. Wearily you drag yourself to your feet and look around for something to help.

The air is thick and the last glimmer of daylight is slipping away. There is a dark cave against the ravine. Fern and moss grow along the sides of the cliff, and willows surround the pool. Could this be the place? No, a voice whispers inside; not yet, this is not your destination.

A long, thick drape of moss hangs near you, and the thought occurs that this velvety cloak might provide some protection from the cold. You pull it down from the rock wall and wrap it around you. The moss robe helps to break the chill. The fern fronds are long enough to weave into a cloak. You gather a few and weave them into a cape to drape around your shoulders; when you finish and try it on, you feel comfortable and warm. Now that you have found comfort, you notice how hungry you are.

A movement on the beach catches your eye. A small water animal has come near and is staring at you. She has something in her mouth. Slowly, you step closer, not wanting to frighten her. She remains calm, and when you are almost within range, she drops a fish in front of you.

"Your dinner," a voice echoes in your head, and then you hear that same laughter you heard earlier, in the stream. The voice is playful, and she motions for you to pick up the fish.

When you do, you find she has sliced it open with her claws and washed it in the pool. The water is clean and clear, and you realize the fish is safe. Carefully you take a small bite. It is juicy and sweet. As you nibble, you feel the life force of this little fish streaming into your body. Suddenly you feel shimmering and sleek, and the energy races through your blood. You thank the fish for its life, for sustaining you, and then turn back to the small animal that provided the nourishment.

She smiles, and her voice echoes, "When you are rested, climb through that cave and you are at your destination." Then, quick as a wink, she disappears. Energy flows through you. You feel strong and ready to continue, so you carefully climb over the rocks and up to the dark opening that awaits you.

The cavern is narrow and high. You feel your way along, running your hand over the wall. Before long, it opens out into a huge room with stalagmites and stalactites glistening with a phosphorescent glow. In the center of the room there is a large pool. The water is black and filled with twinkling lights. There is singing rising from the center, indescribably sweet and alluring. The voices echo off the walls, and your heart begins to pound as you are overcome by the desire to follow the voices.

They swirl around you, reverberating in your mind, and they sing, "Come to us, come to us, leave your home, leave your love, leave your family and ride with us." The pull is so strong you cannot escape and you plunge into the pool, searching for the source of the captivating melody.

As you slide into the water, something begins to happen. You feel strange; your body is shifting and changing. You find yourself transforming into a creature of the water, perhaps a salmon, an otter, a trout, or an octopus. You look at your body to discover what you have become. Feel your body; feel the way the water moves around you now that you do not have to fight to breathe. Play with this for a moment. Notice what it feels like to be a creature of the sea – of the water.

After you adjust to being a creature of the water, you swim deeper and deeper, and follow the current of the pool as it sends you down.

Ahead of you, you see a tunnel in the water, a cave going underneath the cliff, and you follow it. You can still hear the voices singing, filtering through the tunnel.

As you swim through the dark tube, it grows lighter. You swim up and up, heading toward the surface. As you break the waters' edge, you return to human form.

You are near the shore of a large lake, and the forest surrounding this lake shimmers and glows. As you head toward the shore, you wade through the water. Crystals glisten in the sand, and the full moon hangs low overhead, casting its light across the water.

Standing on the shore, you look back at the lake to get an idea of your location. The forest entirely surrounds the lake with a shimmering light. In the center of the lake is a large rock, and you realize that is where the singing begins. This is where you must go.

You slide back into the water. This time, you remain in your human form. As you swim out to the rock, you hope your strength will sustain you long enough to reach your destination.

The shore disappears and the water flows with gentle currents. This seems to help you, guiding you, holding you. The lake lulls you into a bliss that you have never experienced before. It surrounds and warms you. You have a flash back to the time when you lay in your mother's womb, where the fluid cushioned you against the hardships of the outer world. You float for a moment to re-experience that rocking, and remember what it meant to you.

When you return to the task at hand, the water begins to roughen. You shake out of that peaceful calm state. You must remain attentive. You are alert as the water swells and crests, and the waves grow larger. Your muscles begin to ache. You cannot relax.

Now you are closing in on the rock, and the passage becomes more difficult. The waves grow dangerous; and it takes all of your strength. Rain begins to pelt down, stinging as it drives into the surface of the water. The night is so cold now that your muscles start to cramp. The rock is almost within reach.

Again, the water swells with a big wave. The current pushes you to the rock's edge. You pull yourself up; then, with bleeding hands, drag yourself onto the slab of granite. Then, you as rest, you find yourself wrapped in a beautiful warm robe, the color of water.

You lie there for what seems like an infinite amount of time, but eventually you catch your breath and sit up. You see you are not alone on the rock. Circles of women - beautiful, and so ethereal they almost seem formed of the mist, surround you, singing.

In the center stands a grand throne of pearl and amethyst, and on the throne sits a woman cloaked in long ringlets of seaweed. Her hair is the color of twilight, and she wears a gown woven of fog and raindrops. She sits in front of a large bowl, so large you could fit in it, and it is filled with water darker than any you have ever seen.

She motions for you to come close. When you stand at her feet, she says' "I am the Queen of Water. You have come to me." Her voice echoes with the roar of the waterfall.

She continues, "Understand this, I am the force of your body, I am the home from which life began. Your ancestors swam in my primordial seas. I cushion your tears and soothe you with gentle raindrops. But I am also the force of the storm, the wild cresting waves, the roar of the hurricane, the encompassing floodwaters that rise without check. Do not underestimate me or deny my strength."

As she speaks, she shifts her form and a great serpent rises from the water, greater than any serpent ever before known or seen. A voice echoes, "I am the Primordial Mother of the Ocean. Learn of me and pay me respect."

She shifts again and stands cloaked in a golden cover; she is the loveliest woman you have ever seen. "I am the Goddess of Love. Love me and desire me and ride on my waves of passion."

Once more she shifts, and she is wild and fearsome and full of dark storm clouds. " I am the goddess of the angry seas, and I drown sailors who dare to challenge my strength. Do not think you can beat me. I am always more powerful than you."

Then she is back to herself again, and she sits down and smiles gently. "Understand this, I am in each raindrop that falls from the heavens, I am in each teardrop you shed, and when you drink of me, you bring my life force into your body."

She gives you the goblet to keep and says, "Place the water that has been charged by the dark moon in this goblet, and you may touch the sea of knowledge in your dreams." Then she says, "It is time for you to leave." As she speaks, a boat comes, and she bids you board.

The boat glides silently through the water. A great mist rises, and you can no longer see anything beyond the fog. As you glide along in the vapors, the boat suddenly comes to a stop. The mist lifts just a little, and you see a staircase rising from the side of the boat. You cannot see where it goes, but you understand you must climb it. There are 5 stairs.

At the first step you feel the land twist beneath you, and the vibration of Earth races through your body, leaving you rooted.

At the second step, you feel the air whip around you and the vibration races through your mind, leaving you cleansed and alert.

At the third step, you feel the flames crackle around you, and the vibration of fire races though your blood, leaving you full of desire.

At the fourth step, you feel the water rushing around you, and the vibration of water races through your heart, leaving you hearing the voices of your inner mind.

At the fifth step, you find yourself balanced between light and dark, the vibration of all elements mingling in your body.

As you come back – you will become awake and alert and the feeling of balance will stay with you as you go about your daily life.

ଵଵଵଵଵ

Water is the element that gives us movement, the ebb and flow of life. It brings motion to the solid earth. It is the flow of our emotions that moves us along the journey of life with its ups and downs. It is during the emotional times that spark creativity of the arts and procreation.

Questions

What have you learned from these meditations?

How will you look at the element of water differently?

How will you look at yourself differently?

What has changed? Will you do anything differently?

How do you feel the water element works inside of you?

What thoughts do you have about the Sacral Chakra?

When do you think it would be helpful to "pull in" the energy of the sacral chakra?

How could that help you in life situations?

ഗ൪ഗ൪

FIRE – South – Summer

The Ethereal Body

If there is no fire or spark or passion –

(There is NO LIFE.)

Summer is the time of fun, celebration, love and joy. The days are long. The farmers are collecting the harvest and food is plentiful. In the Corporate World, it is the time of hard work and reaching for the goals, bringing in business. It is the time of getting things done while we have many hours of light.

Definition of FIRE: (Dictionary)

1) The phenomenon of combustion

   revealed in light, flame, heat

2) One of the 4 elements of the alchemists

3) Burning passion (ardor)

4) Liveliness of imagination (inspiration)

Affirmation:

Come to me Fire, so warm and so bright,
As I walk through life, my pathway do light.
Send me passion to live and love with pure zest,
Standing up for truth when put to the test.

BY THE PASSION OF HER SOULS DESIRE
BY DANCING FLAMES AND BURNING FIRES

CLEANSE AND CLEAR MY BODY CLEAN BURN AWAY ALL NEGATIVITY

About:

Fire is dynamic and unmanageable. In its positive form it presents as creativity and action, as a force persistently striving upwards, willing to take chances and make leaps of faith. In its negative form it is destructive, oppressive, impulsive and prideful. It consumes and reduces to ashes all within its path when uncontrolled. It has the capacity to consume itself and is vulnerable to extinction when its sources of fuel are insufficient. To a certain extent, it is the element most identified with man and his power over Nature.

Astrology: Fire

Fire tends to go up, and can raise things beyond the clouds. The sun and the stars are fire. They sit high in the sky! Fire cannot truly be confined, although it can be controlled. Even so, it escapes into the sky. Not surprisingly, fire is associated with spirit, high ideals. Fire ideas can be very distant from the ideas of Earth. While fire consumes, it also creates new life (forest fires remove the old and enable the new - some plants even wait for the fire to release their seeds). Of all the elements, fire captures our attention the most.

Fire is raw energy.

Fire people have high spirits, self-confidence, enthusiasm, direct honesty and openness. They project a radiant, vitalizing energy that glows warmly. They need a good deal of freedom for expression. They are consumed - even entranced - by whatever they do. They are motivated by excitement, insight and intuition. That is, they get an idea that captivates them. They do not consider rational or logical thinking or practical feasibility. The idea comes to them fully formed and full of power. While the idea may grow over a period of time, it does not grow logically but intuitively. Sometimes fiery people do not know why they must do what they must do!

Fire appears as if from nowhere, it grabs everyone's attention, and forces its way through almost everything, consuming the air, evaporating the water and charring the earth.

Not surprisingly, fire people are assertive, individualistic, active and self-expressive. Fire sign energies can stimulate others, but they can also overpower and exhaust them. Good natured and fun loving, they may have many friends. They are generous with their time, energy, and resources. They value having a good time above material possessions. Fire people may believe so strongly in their own powers and abilities that they fail to notice the powers and abilities of others.

They belong to a group that is the most daring and capable inspiring natural leaders. They lead from the front. In war or business, they are out in the front leading the way. They are independent and individualistic leaders, rarely consulting others before they act. In fact, they may not even think things through to themselves, because their mode of thought is intuitive. They are always "on stage" and need to be recognized and admired for their attainment and accomplishments. They consider being appreciated more important than being rich. Nothing hurts them more than being ignored. The fire sign's sense of honesty is straightforward and often child-like. They believe everyone is like them - an open book. This may lead them to be gullible and naive, or to others exploiting their openness.

Chakra:

Fire relates to the 3rd Chakra – the Solar Plexus, the center of personal power. It is associated with identity and self esteem. It is the power center for assertiveness, intuition and inner drive. It controls digestion and the metabolic systems, processing energy and providing the "spark" to overcome apathy and inertia.

NOTE: Find a quiet spot, relax, and take 3 deep breaths to calm the mind, body and spirit. Read slowly and pause often.

Meditation: Solar Plexus Chakra

Allow your awareness to flow to the middle of your body, imagine a dual coil of vibrant energy embracing and dancing around your spine and body. As one spiral comes down from above and fills body with the spirit of life; there is another spiral that pulls up the power of earth to meet the light above. Imagine your entire existence as a reflection of the balance and play of these two energies, flowing and glowing, on and in and around your body. And, breathe. Be sensitive and aware of all thoughts and feelings that may arise as you gently allow the energy center to open, and flow, and swirl. As you proceed – previous blocks and past issues may release to your awareness. Accept whatever happens, reject nothing, surrender yourself, and enjoy the experience. Let us begin.

Place your hands in front of your abdomen, slightly above the waist. Let your fingers join at the tops, all pointing out from your body. Cross the thumbs. Keep the fingers straight. Perhaps you may quietly chant "RAM".

Let awareness linger there without purpose or expectation or intention as the awareness gently stimulates this area, the base of personal power, located in the middle of your body. Whatever present condition; accept it as it is. Acceptance allows this area relax more and more. It starts to turn a circular flow of warm energy. The color is yellow. The energy from below is warming up. Picture a glowing orange ember being fanned with each breath you take, until a warm yellow flame appears. Feel the radiant heat from within. Just as the light of the rising sun, the warmth increases, filling the body with its soothing glow. A golden warmth touches you from within and completely relaxes you. Surrender to the golden glow. The light reaches down to the greatest depths of your soul, filled with bright clarity. Shadows and tensions dissolve. From the center, light permeates the body until only peace, strength, and abundance abide within you. Golden waves from within radiate out to enfold you in a room of shimmering light. The place has turned to a golden yellow light.

Imagine that your breath comes not through your nose, but directly from the belly. Feel the air flowing into your abdomen. As you connect to this glowing power center, sense the force within that moves your breath in and out. Allow that rhythm to determine depth and pace of breathing and feel how it gently affects the surrounding areas. Continue letting all your stomach muscles relax. Feel the belly. This fire energy center controls breathing and digestion, as oxygen and nutrients stimulate and release body heat. The belly center; this is the source of your personal power. It is linked to your body's "fight or flight" mechanism and reflects your dynamics to the outside world: whether you feel vulnerable or trusting; in control or afraid; if you fear - if you are anxious, defensive or aggressive. So, tell your body that you are in a safe secure place and let your belly become soft. Every time you let out a breath, release all muscle tension, along with all other protective feelings. Your belly is the center of control and trust. At the "gut level" we learn to separate between friend and foe, pain and pleasure and to respond accordingly.

You may repeat the affirmation –

- My power radiates from the center of my being.

- I am worthy of the very best in life.

- I am strong, centered and determined.

- I am powerful, brave and focused.

Bathe in this clear, yellow vibration and allow it to flow in and around and through your body. Pause and ponder.

And, now it is time to return, to this place and time and day. Bring yourself back slowly. When you are ready, open your eyes.

ଅଇଇଇ

Meditation for the Fire Element*

You decide to take a journey to the element of Fire. You are standing on a dry, dusty road. In front of you there is a forest of tall, thick trees. It is nighttime, almost midnight. There is a small beam of moonlight to light your way. The air is warm and you can feel a gentle breeze against your skin. The forest and the trees entice you to enter. Before you enter this mysterious forest, you ask permission of the trees, the night, and Mother Nature.

As you meander quietly along the path, you can smell the aroma from the trees. It is a blend of oak, cedar and pine. Occasionally there are vines that hang from the branches. Once inside, there is a tingling of electricity and chill bumps run up and down your arms. It is as if a magic spell has taken over you and it is soothing you into a drowsy, hazy fog. Yet, you feel no fear or danger. It feels as if a great power is guiding and watching over you.

You continue to quietly stroll deeper into the forest, observing everything along the path. It seems as though your senses have been intensified because everything around you is enhanced and magnified. The sounds around you are clear and distinct. Even the smallest movements catch your attention. It is almost as if you could pass through here blindfolded because you are so aware of the sounds and movements and aromas that guide you along.

Then you sense that there is someone close, following you. You stop. You look around. Behind you there is a ball of light — floating in the air, glowing with green iridescent energy, the color of glistening, shimmering, shining emeralds.

A voice echoes, "I am your guide in this part of your journey." and you realize the sound is coming from the light. "I am a night flame of faerie fire, no need to be afraid. You must pass through the faerie fire to complete your journey to the element of Fire. Follow me. Do not linger, for the faeries are quick to catch and trick the innocent."

Next, there is a shiny glistening sparkle on the trees, their auras glowing and shining bright. "It always is this way; for now you are allowed to see it," says the light. It is as if the light hears your thoughts. Up ahead, there is a dark spot among the trees. As you approach, a shiver runs through your body and your mind trembles, for there is a stirring of power all around you. You feel something very ancient, very primal, and very close by. You tiptoe forward and gaze in the dark space between the trees.

The black is the darkness of the void. It hypnotizes you with its incredible depth. After a moment of gazing, you begin to see a swirl of sparkling color - a spiral of light, and it gradually becomes two glowing red eyes that pierce the darkness. The red eyes pierce into you, delving into the inner part of you. They are strong and watchful, and intense.

"The red eyes in the forest at midnight," whispers the light. "They belong to the Hunter, the Heart of the Forest; he lives in the faerie fire. Watch your step when crossing the woods at night, for he is always watching you."

You move further into the forest, listening to the birds hovering around you. The path turns to the right. The light floats along and comes to a fork in the road. You follow the light. You must be careful for the slope is steep. You notice that it leads down to a beach. At one point, you must slide because the land is too steep to walk. When you reach the bottom, you find yourself along the shore of a small inlet that kisses the land. The water is so very beautiful, shining in the night; it shimmers with lights of green, blue, pink and yellow.

With a rush of delight, you run to the water, drawn in by the glittering, shimmering lights. With every step, sparks light the sand. You stop and press your hands on the ground. They are covered with sparkles. Suddenly you are lighthearted, laughing and full of joy. The delight in your heart is overwhelming. You dance on the sand and watch the sparks fly over and around you. Then you wade into the water, where the sparkles glitter and it feels like you are walking and wading and splashing and twirling among the stars.

Then, the voice begins to speak, "The faerie fire is a mysterious thing. There are no words to explain the depths of this happiness, the intoxication, yet it exists. It is real. Now come back, there is another stop before I leave you."

You return to the path, full of the phosphorescent sparkles of faerie fire. They remain within your heart and memory. The light guides you along the path until you see a purple fire dancing across the road.

"When you pass through the purple fire, you will find a fine layer of ash covering your body. The wind will blow it away, and with it will go pain and anger and any old bonds that chain you. The purple rays are hotter than flame, hotter than fire, and they burn through to your core and leave you pure and new. Then you are ready to continue your journey. After the purple fire, you will find a green fire. This flame is the purest essence of the faerie fire. You must pass through it to continue your quest. Good luck and good bye." And the light fades into the night.

When you pass through the purple flame, a fine layer of ash covers your body. The breeze sweeps up and blows it away. Beneath the ash, your skin is new and clear and your heart feels lighter.

The forest comes to an end, and there the green flame is waiting. Take one last look behind you, and then run though the green flame - the green fire of the forest.

It crackles around you, sparkling and magnetic. It resonates inside you as your body shifts and changes. You move with more grace in the fire, as it slides up your arms and legs, seeping into your belly; sensuous, it leaves you breathless and waiting.

You discover you can shape yourself; you can change as you wish. Do you want to be taller? Thinner? Do you want to radiate confidence or strength? The faerie fire will change whatever you like. When you are complete, step through and look at yourself to see the changes.

When you look up again you notice that you are at the edge of an open meadow. The grass is thick, then turns sparse up ahead, and you notice a shimmer of dawn rising in the east. The path slopes upward - a gentle, easy incline. You follow the path and continue your journey as the night turns to day and the stars fade from the sky.

It looks like the day will be hot. There are no clouds in the sky, and the forest has become a distant memory. The path is long and dusty. The grass is sparse; the dirt is dry. Cracks splinter the ground; no rain has fallen here for a long time. The sun is now above the horizon and it is hot, as you had anticipated.

As you look around, it seems there is only the desert, with a few scattered stones. After a while your feet become hot and weary. You find a large rock nearby and sit. As you rest, there is a rustling noise close by. You look down to see a large lizard is sitting there, patiently watching you.

He is red with stripes of orange, and his golden eyes stare up at you. A long tongue forks out. In a whistling voice, "I am your guide. You need a walking stick." He waves his tongue toward a low, long rock near you. Underneath you find a walking stick that is perfect for you.

"Follow me," he says. The lizard leads you up the path, which has become much steeper. As you climb, your muscles ache and burn; yet you understand that you must keep moving. Finally, when you think you can go no further, you reach the top. There is a mountain ahead. Dark, with streaks of rust-colored rocks trailing down its side, the mountain is formed of black lava that flowed out of its cone long, long ago.

The hardened lava lies in waves, pillows of rock, thick and glistening with volcanic glass. Strange shapes and silhouettes stand frozen over the land. The ancient flow goes on for miles. As you start, you find that the path is gone. You must cross the hard lava. Utilizing the walking stick, you forge ahead, slowly working around the twisted rock. You must be careful here, for the lava is sharp and full of rough edges.

The taste of sulfur fills your mouth, and you must stop for water. As you climb higher and higher up the side of the mountain, steam rises from cracks in the lava around you. This place shows massive destruction. Yet out of that destruction, new land is born; nutrients weather down and feed the soil, and plants grow again.

You curve around the side of the mountain; when you look over the edge of the worn path, you see a drop, maybe two hundred feet down, into a lake of lava. The lava boils and turns, and the twisting tongues of flame dance on its surface. At first, terrifying, and then mesmerizing; it churns constantly as you watch.

The path twists and turns away from the lava. It curves around the black mountain. You wander into what once was a forest. The trees are now black – like charcoal; they protrude out of the ash that covers the land.

Fire is like a dual-edged sword. At its most constructive, it burns brightly; it drives us onward and feeds our creativity and passion. But when it turns destructive, it consumes all, leaving only the ashes behind. Never underestimate the power of the flames; what might seem like a single spark can flare up into a raging inferno if the energy is not directed, focused, or given boundaries.

When you shade your eyes against the sun and look out to the horizon, there is an enormous fountain, carved from the lava. It sits in a meadow of ash. The fountain is covered with flames and glowing heat. In the center, there is a woman bathing. Her skin is of purest crimson, her hair streaming bright cherry red. Her eyes mirror the brilliance of the sun. Surely, her gaze will blind you if you meet it directly. She motions to you to come close.

When you approach, the heat intensifies until it feels like tiny blisters will bubble up on your skin. The woman holds up her hand to stop you. Sensuously her body changes shape in the flame and the passions that throb just below the surface reach out to encompass you. She speaks, "I am the Queen of Fire, hold out your hand, feel my power."

At first, you feel a warm glow – the warmth of a spring morning, the warmth of a summer breeze against your skin. Then the heat intensifies. It becomes the heat of the woodstove, warming you on crisp autumn evening. It changes again. You feel the crackle of bonfires and the smell of burning wood; then, the heat becomes the sweltering heat of noon on a summer's day, and sweat pours down on your face.

"I am passion," she says. "I am the creative force that refuses to be subdued. Try to suppress me. I will rise up and burn you to ashes. Embrace me, use me with prudence, and I am your greatest ally. I heal with my golden rays. And, with my molten rock that pours from the core of the earth, I destroy. My destruction makes way for new creation. This cycle has repeated itself from the beginning of time." You pause and ponder these words.

"This is not a place for mortals. The heat will burn you. Go now; there is a path beyond this fountain. Follow it and it will lead you home."

You follow the path; it leads you down a slope. The sun is now lower in the sky. The lizard waves and bids you farewell. The walking becomes a little easier, the ash thins out, and there are fewer and fewer of the stunted trees.

As you proceed down the hill, blades of grass begin to peek through the soil. The open path continues by a low cliff, and then leads to the shore below.

You twist and turn. The walking is easy and pleasant after your time in the land of fire. At the shore, there is a horse waiting, saddled. The horse seems to feel your exhaustion, so the ride is slow, easy and gentle.

You ride for what seems hours. The horse takes the fork in road and travels through the late evening on a path that is gradually ascends a hill. At the top of the slope, just before twilight, the horse stops to let you off. There are 10 steps in front of you, the place where you began your journey. The horse has brought you back exactly where you started.

Home once again.

And now, it is time to return to this day and this time. Bring yourself back slowly. When ready, you may open your eyes.

&.&.&.&

SUMMARY: When I think of fire, I think of
passion, I think of light. When we come out of
darkness, there is light. We cannot touch it, yet
what is life without it. Many people shut down
with the hurt and pain of life. They do not
physically die, yet the spark of life, the passion
that drives us to feel (water), to breathe (air), to
manifest the things we enjoy (earth) – that is
where it all begins. God said, "Let there be
light". We are all light beings in this world –
special, unique and wonderful. Let your light
shine unto us all.

Questions:

What have you learned from these meditations?

How will you look at the element of fire differently?

How will you look at yourself differently?

What has changed?   Will you do anything differently?

How do you feel the fire element works inside of you?

When do you think is a good time to sit and be with the "Solar Plexus Chakra"?

When do you think it would be helpful to "pull in" the energy of the Solar Plexus chakra?

How could that help you in life situations?

AIR – East – Spring

The Mental Body

We survive MINUTES without air

(3 - 8 minutes)

In spring, it is the time of new beginnings. The dark days of winter are over, it is time to get outside, enjoy the sun and plant the seeds of the year. It is the time of setting goals, and dreams and making a plan. The farmers are busy preparing the soil for the new crops. In the Corporate World, it is the time of delivering projects to the staff, staff reviews, setting goals, and training.

Definition of AIR: (Dictionary)

1) Breath

2) Mixture of invisible odorless gases that surround the earth

3) A light breeze

4) Empty space, nothingness

Affirmation:

Come to me Air, so fresh and so clean,
Grant me the wisdom to be sharp and keen.
Send me creativity and clarity too;
Bring positive thoughts to all that I do.

BY HER FRAGRANT BREATH, THE AIR
BY WINDS BLOWN COLD AND BREEZES FAIR
CLEANSE AND CLEAR MY BODY CLEAN
BLOW AWAY ALL NEGATIVITY

About:

This element is about the intellect and rational thought. It is represented by the double-edged sword of justice, so-called because of the power of thought can heal or destroy. Like a surgeon's knife, when wielded with reason it has the power to discriminate and separate the good from the evil, to cut out diseased flesh and leave the healthy intact. When guided by

128

passion and emotions it has the potential for great destruction, as if by virtue of its keenness can do infinitely more and deeper damage than that of a blunt object.

Astrology: Air

Since air is light, it pervades everything on earth. For a long way into the sky and even in deep caves there is air. Air rises, but not as much as fire. Like fire, air is difficult to control or to capture. It is free. Yet it links everything to everything else. Air is associated with words and language. Language and speech require air. It has a serial quality. You can blow air from one position to another. For example, you can direct the breath to blow away some dust - the air moves from the mouth to the position of the dust. Language requires that words are uttered in a particular sequence, and the basis of logic is within language. (You cannot prove logic) For most of human history, the air was a mode force of transportation (sailing ships) and a major source of power (windmills).

It loves freedom, and if captured, it will escape at the first opportunity. (If you capture it in a balloon, it will seep out or explode out whenever it can). Air is also associated with the interrelationships (links) between people and things.

So one keyword is "linking":

- Logic links ideas,
- Language links words,
- Transportation links places, and
- Words link ideas

In order to link ideas together, we need to use abstraction to some degree. So like fire, air can be abstract. Although air is everywhere, it remains air. It does unite with things in the world, but not as fast as fire. So the air can be objective and a bit impersonal. It is social because it is everywhere, but the associations are not as deep as those of water, or as lasting as those of earth.

Air people are concerned with thought, ideas and intellect. They are detached and objective. Yet they might not accomplish their goals unless they are grounded in earth. They are the theory people in the "theory versus practice" debate. They can become dreamers, thinking and planning, but not applying. Air people are reflective and think things through logically before they implement their ideas. They can be procrastinators, but they rarely make mistakes through lack of thought. They tend not to be emotional, but fair-minded. They are group-oriented rather than person-oriented. They love humanity, but are not that close to individuals. They have varied interests and could become perpetual students.

Chakra:

Air is related to the Heart Chakra, along with unconditional love. For this document, a better example is the fifth chakra, or Throat Chakra. It is ether and it represents communication, thought, and creativity that correlate to the Throat Chakra. The throat chakra associated with sound and creative self-expression, speech and communication; the ability to speak honestly and connect with our inner truth. It is the center of transformation and change.

NOTE: The Heart Chakra is associated with air and unconditional love. I am taking the liberty to use the Throat Chakra as a representation of communication and creativity that is also higher level of air. Find a quiet spot; take a few deep breaths to relax body, mind and spirit. Read slowly and pause often.

MEDITATION: Chakra for Throat

As you sit, imagine a dual coil of vibrant energy embracing and dancing around your spine and body. As one spiral comes down from above and fills body with the spirit of life; there is another spiral that pulls up the power of earth to meet the light above. Imagine your entire existence as a reflection of the balance and play of these two energies, flowing and glowing, on and in and around your body. And, breathe. Be sensitive and aware of all thoughts and feelings that may arise as you gently allow the energy center to open, and flow, and swirl. As you proceed – previous blocks and past issues may arise to your awareness. Accept whatever happens, reject nothing, surrender yourself, and enjoy the experience. Let us begin.

Let your awareness move to the area of the throat - become aware without purpose, intention or expectation. As you focus your awareness to your throat, it stimulates the area.

Cross your fingers on the inside of your hands, without thumbs. Let the thumbs touch at the tops, and pull up slightly. Hum or chant "HAM".

Become aware of an infinitely fine vibration - a subtle frequency that gives rise to a clear blue radiance. Allow the radiant vibrations to expand from you until you become unlimited, like the sky that accommodates with ALL that is - just like infinite space, you encompass sun and stars and all life.

You allow all life to flow within, to the oneness of your own being. You accept ALL - as it is. You let ALL come and go in this infinite freedom. Bliss vibrates within you. Listen to the infinite vibration of space. Allow yourself to become a channel for all messages received from the innermost part of you... Hold the air and vibration in for a moment while relaxing... take in more. And, relax.

Each time you exhale; feel the radiant energy at the base of your neck and throughout your lungs. The color is light sky blue. The element is pure thought. In the throat area, we truly discover the power of the mind - the importance of the soul-dream. This is the seat of creativity and self-healing.

The thyroid is the regulator of the endocrine glands and hormones and immune system. Send the message from your mind to your body that all systems may now be in perfect balance. Visualize a crystal blue light shining through your neck and throat, clearing and cleansing out any and all limitation, negativity, and fear.

Soften this area, from the jaw to shoulders. The "voice" center controls your communication, artistic wisdom, and the capacity for creativity.

See yourself, as you are - a sensitive, creative being, with a contribution to the world. This is who and what you truly are. The medium of the mind is higher thought and symbolic knowledge.

The dynamics are subtle, philosophical and reflective. Invoke your sense of purpose and highest aspiration. Bring to mind the example and inspiration of your teachers. As you physically and psychically "open", recognize yourself as creative person, with ability to speak truth and to respond authentically to ideas and to create and appreciate BEAUTY itself.

Picture, in your mind, a pure crystal chalice filled with a brilliant, blue light. From its center, a magnificent white dove emerges, spreads her wings, and lifts into the sky with breathtaking grace. You feel blessed by the vision. And, then, you realize – this is you.   And, Breathe.

You may repeat to yourself the following affirmations –

- I am able to celebrate the beauty in my life.
- I am able and willing to speak my truth.
- I am able to hear and communicate the voice of my soul.
- I release the negativity in my life to make room for my true voice.

Rest in these thoughts; allow these words to soak in. Pause and ponder.

And, now it is time to return, to this place and time and day. Bring yourself back slowly. When you are ready, open your eyes.

ଡ଼ଡ଼ଡ଼ଡ଼

Meditation for the Element of Air*

You have decided to take a journey to visit the element of Air.

You are standing outside, near an open cliff, overlooking a valley below. It is just before dawn. The early morning sky is a pale blue that fades into a sweet dusty rose as the sun is making its way above the horizon. It is cool and comfortable as you gaze at the sky. There are strands of clouds that float by, distant and barely moving. They will soon burn off with the heat of the morning sun.

You step to the edge of the cliff and stretch your hands out to the Eastern sky. You whisper, "Wind of the East! Come to me." As the voice fades, you close your eyes and feel the east wind against your skin.

In the distance, you hear laughter. A burst of air sweeps up around you. It is a cloud of air that appears almost human. The cool, crisp breeze of morning accompanies him and he laughs, again. With each breath it seems like cobwebs and dust are blowing away with the breeze of his voice.

"I rule the East Wind. Touch me and feel my power." You reach out and touch his hand. As your fingers penetrate the wind, suddenly, your mind becomes more alert and aware. You feel clear-headed. Your thoughts become rapid and rational. Everything seems brighter and smells cleaner. As the breeze rushes through you, it cleans away any sluggish energy that is within you. A rush of excitement snaps you to attention.

"The East wind has the power to cleanse you, to free you from old habits. I am the air of new beginnings. I am the wind of thought and communication." With a rush, he is gone. With that, you take a nice deep breath to let the East wind settle into your being, as you inhale in this experience of the wind.

You turn to face the South and call out into the clear blue sky. "Wind of the South, come to me now." Shortly you feel the air change. It is now the breeze of a hot summer day. It feels hot and steamy.

You stand briefly to catch your balance, when you hear laughter like thunder, huge and bellowing. The spirit that approaches comes in like a hot, crackling wind. You feel the hairs on your arms stand on end. "Welcome," his voice echoes. "Feel my power and my light!" You reach out to touch the South Wind. As your fingers meet his, the wind sweeps around you and crackles — like lightning on a hot summer night. You feel your mind shoot up with passion, the passion to act and create. You see stories, and poems, and pictures, creativity - they are all here. You feel words swirling, just waiting for you to create something. Your body shivers; this wind is sensuous. It plays gently, caressing and teasing you like hundreds of fingers tracing tattoos on your skin.

"I am the wind of creativity, the wind that brings you the scent of fresh mowed grass where you lay with your beloved. I am the wind that precedes lightning." You rest and simmer in the heat. You dream of things to create, your passions in life, the things you love. After a moment you hear. "Now, you must go." And with a rush, he is gone...

You turn to the West and call out, "Wind of the West come to me now!"

Once again, you feel the wind change. The heat is gone. You see dark clouds approaching, the sky turns gloomy and the air turns cool. Soon another wind spirit rumbles up to meet you. His face is mournful. He remains melancholy, yet seems at peace with himself and the world. "I am the West wind, I bid you to feel my power and stay as long as you need." You reach out and you are swept into the storm. The rain pounds around you, this wind is wet and it blows cool against your skin. It whispers of peace and quiet. It speaks of turning inward to look at the inner you. It blows through your life and cleanses you of old wounds. It brings the rain of autumn to clear the air and make way for the frost.

"Behold," he says, "I am the West wind. I bring you the joy and the sadness of the heart. I blow into your life when mist is needed to comfort you and I bring the fog to protect you from sight. I am the wind of autumn and of the beautiful sunset when the air is cool and when birds fly gently home. I bring fertility and I bring peace." He drifts off, leaving you alone, again. Now, the next step of your quest is waiting for you.

And, again you stand on the edge of the cliff. You turn to face the North and raise your hands to your mouth. "North Wind – rushing and mighty! Come!"

This cloud turns darker still. A bitter chill sweeps down as the wind whirls up around you, swirling with snowflakes and the Ruler of the North Wind, stands gravely before you.

"Behold, I am the Ruler of the North Wind. I welcome you and extend to you the knowledge of my land." The wind comes sweeping around you; a howling storm of ferocity that brings with it deep snow and death and the darkness of a winter night.

"I bring with me sleep - the wind that clears the trees of their leaves and the wind that cries out, destroying old patterns and habits that lie in my path. I clear depression and anxiety and envy from your heart, leaving a space to be filled by new breezes of the East."

"Understand that without me, there would be no beginning, for there must be an end to all things before new life can begin. I guard the road of the dead; and, ghosts live in my memories. Leave them to me; free yourself of your chains. I will sweep them away."

And now, he looks at you and says, "You must attend the last stage of your journey. Call my name if you need me. Yet be aware, I will come." Sparkling with frost, he glides off into the night.

You stand at the edge of the cliff and realize you have made the circuit of the four directions, with only the center remaining. As you watch, a strong wind comes along. It carries you aloft, far higher than you have ever been. You are dizzy with flight, spinning and whirling in the air.

You find yourself on the edge of a rainbow. Slowly, you hop down. As you do, you hear the sweet singing of chimes in the wind and you turn to see a woman dressed in colors of pale blue and lavender, with golden threads woven through the silken veils. She wears a necklace of diamonds and her hair is pulled back, covered with a net of spiders' web to keep it neat.

"Welcome." You hear the echo of spring, the call of early morning. "I am the Queen of Air." She invites you to sit on the rainbow bridge; then, she sits beside you, a bouquet of white daisies in her hand. "You have journeyed far to learn about the element of Air. So I will tell you of the element of the East. Understand – without air, there is no life. Without my breath, you cease to exist. Without me, this world would be but a lifeless orb floating in space. I am essential, as are all elements, for survival."

"I am mist and fog and vapors trailing in the wind. I am the wind and the breeze and the still currents of air on a hot summer's night. Without me, fire would not exist, the earth would bear no life and the water could support no fish."

After a moment, she reaches out and helps you to your feet. You feel the cool promise of morning calling you to rise from the bed for a new day is waiting. "Slide down the rainbow" she says. "It will take you home." And she is gone.

You look at the rainbow. It is steep yet very wide and when you sit down on it; you find it feels safe. You push off with your hands and find yourself speeding down the arc, watching as you slide downward.

You take a deep breath to calm yourself, for you are traveling at a speed faster than thought. And you begin to count ...each beat brings you closer to the earth below. You see clouds as they slip past you – racing by... Your speed begins to slow a bit. You can see the rainbow curving toward the earth below. You can see the tops of the trees and you slow even more. You see the cliffs where you started your journey. You are almost at the bottom of the rainbow. You slide to the ground and turn; the rainbow fades in the early morning. The sun is rising in the East, as you welcome the new day.

And, now it is time to return, to this place and time and day. Bring yourself back slowly. When you are ready, open your eyes.

ଧ୍ୟଧ୍ୟଧ୍ୟଧ୍ୟ

Air is something we cannot see or touch. Yet, it is everywhere. It surrounds everything we do. It supports life. It is the veil that clouds our vision. It is the wind clears dust and debris to bring clarity. It is a dual edged sword.

Questions:

What have you learned from these meditations?

How will you look at the element of air differently?

How will you look at yourself differently?

What has changed? Will you do anything differently?

How do you feel the air element works inside of you?

What thoughts do you have about the Throat Chakra?

When do you think it would be helpful to "pull in" the energy of the Throat chakra?

How could that help you in life situations?

ನನನನ

*The Element Meditations (Earth, Water, Air and Fire): inspired by the Magical Mediations, by Yasmine Galenorn

CHAPTER 6 - Epilogue

These meditations have helped me experience life at an elemental (earth, water, fire, air) and vibrational (chakra) level. They all work together to make something whole (complete). By understanding each of these, it becomes a game of intertwining and growing and learning the ebb and flow of each, when to use them for your benefit and when to control them, instead of them controlling you. It is up to YOU to manage the orchestra.

Something my mother told me, "Remember, as you go through life. NO ONE cares more about you than you." At the time, I thought that was a silly thing to say to me. As the years have passed, I think it is very wise. When I care for myself, do what is right in my heart, do what "feels" right; that is when life "flows" and all is well. It is when I resist and think too much or listen to others (outside of what my heart tells me) – that is when I trip and fall over those sticks and stones.

All life revolves around a circle, never ending. "When one door closes, another one opens." It is darkest, just before dawn, a new day, a new breath, a new life, a new chapter in life. It is when we learn to live in the moment, for the moment, everything gets brighter and life moves on. That is the blessing.

Hopefully, this document has helped you along your journey as you seek happiness. I like the word bliss. It has a feeling of happiness and contentment and feeling good with one's self. For that is the only way to truly find happiness in whatever form. To me, happiness is a fleeting thing – bliss is heaven on earth.

My blessings I send to you. May you cherish every moment of life, for every moment has a blessing in it, sometimes joy, and sometimes growth, or sometimes challenge - all good.

My favorite prayer!!
Imagine for a moment
What it would feel like,
To lay your head in the hands of God.
Imagine feeling the profound tranquility
Bathed in Ecstasy
That would drench your entire soul,
If you were to rest your head
In the hands of your creator,
And to bow your heavily burdened forehead
Onto the doorstep of the Divine
You would inhale a fragrance so magnificent
That the aroma of bliss
Would permeate your entire being,
You would shimmer in a light so scintillating
That you would recognize it
As the beauty of your own soul
If...

You were to lay your head in the hands of God.

~ Gurumayi Chidvalasananda

Books used for reference:

- Wheels of Light, a Study of the Chakras, Rosalyn Bruyere

- Moonlight, Secrets of Energy, Silver Ravenwolf

- The Power of a Broken-Heart Open, Julie Interrante

- Magical Meditations, Yasmine Galenorn

- The Craft, Dorothy Morrison

- The Chakra Deck, Olivia Miller

- The Only Way to Learn Astrology, Marion March & Joan McEvers

- Wikipedia – my favorite friend and companion when writing.

Appendix – books used in research

- Living Buddha, Living Christ, Thich Nhat Hanh

- The Wiccan Year, Judy Ann Nock

- Meditations for Healing, Larry Moen

- Guided Meditations, Explorations, and Healings, Stephen Levine

- Minding the Body, Mending the Mind, Joan Borysenko, PhD

- My Voice Will Go With You, Milton Erickson

- Many Lives, Many Masters, Brian Weiss

Audio Recordings of the Meditations are available for purchase:

1. EARTH
2. WATER
3. AIR
4. FIRE
5. Root Chakra
6. Sacral Chakra
7. Solar Plexus
8. Heart Chakra
9. Throat Chakra
10. Brow Chakra
11. Crown Chakra

Contact: vraylong2@aol.com

Namaste'

36654453R00090

Printed in Great Britain
by Amazon